United States Presidents

Andrew Jackson

Anne Welsbacher
ABDO Publishing Company

visit us at
www.abdopub.com

Published by ABDO Publishing Company, 4940 Viking Drive, Edina, Minnesota 55435.
Copyright © 1999 by Abdo Consulting Group, Inc. International copyrights reserved in
all countries. No part of this book may be reproduced in any form without written
permission from the publisher.

Published 1999
Printed in the United States of America.
Second printing 2002

Cover Photo and Interior Photo credits: Archive Photos, Corbis-Bettmann, AP/Wide World

Edited by Lori Kinstad Pupeza
Contributing editor: Brooke Henderson

Library of Congress Cataloging-in-Publication Data

Welsbacher, Anne, 1955-
    Andrew Jackson / Anne Welsbacher.
        p. cm. -- (United States presidents)
    Includes index.
    Summary: Examines the childhood, political career, and other activities of the
seventh president of the United States, the first president to come from a poor family.
        ISBN 1-56239-811-3
        1. Jackson, Andrew, 1767-1845--Juvenile literature. 2. Presidents--United
States--Biography--Juvenile literature. [1. Jackson, Andrew, 1767-1845.
    2. Presidents.] I. Title. II. Series: United States presidents (Edina, Minn.)
    E382.W45 1998
    973.5'6'092--dc21
    [B]   98-10140
                                                                        CIP
                                                                         AC

Revised Edition 2002

Contents

"Old Hickory"

*A*ndrew Jackson was the seventh president of the United States. He was the first president to come from a poor family. Many people liked him for being common, like them.

Andrew Jackson was hurt in battles and had many terrible diseases but he always kept fighting. For this reason, people called him "Old Hickory." Hickory wood is one of the hardest, toughest kinds of wood.

As a boy in South Carolina, Andrew Jackson was wild. He liked to get in fights, and had a bad temper. He did not like school.

Andrew joined the army to fight in the American Revolution. He suffered from **smallpox** and other hardships during and after that war.

A statue of Andrew Jackson on his horse at the Tennessee State Capitol in Nashville

When he grew older, Andrew decided to settle down and be a lawyer. He had a good law practice in Tennessee and other new states.

Later, Andrew Jackson and Rachel Donelson Robards were married. They built a home and added land to their **plantation**. He loved his family.

Andrew Jackson was a leader in **politics**, but he did not like the job. He went back to farming at his plantation.

Andrew Jackson fought in the War of 1812 against Great Britain. The war changed his life. He became a national hero because of the battles he led.

Andrew Jackson was elected president in 1828. While he was president, he and other leaders broke many promises he made to Native Americans. He forced many to leave their lands and move west.

Andrew Jackson was president for two terms. Then he went home to his plantation in Tennessee. He died at age 78 on June 8, 1845.

President Andrew Jackson, the 7th president of the U.S. is shown in an undated portrait.

Andrew Jackson (1767-1845)
Seventh President

BORN:	March 15, 1767
PLACE OF BIRTH:	Waxhaw, South Carolina
ANCESTRY:	Scottish Irish
FATHER:	Andrew Jackson (?-1767)
MOTHER:	Elizabeth Hutchinson Jackson (?-1781)
WIFE:	Rachel Donelson Robards (1767-1828)
CHILDREN:	One boy (adopted)
EDUCATION:	Attended public schools; studied law in Salisbury, North Carolina
RELIGION:	Presbyterian
OCCUPATION:	Lawyer, soldier, congressman
MILITARY SERVICE:	Judge Advocate of Davidson County Militia (1791); Major General of Tennessee Militia (1802-1812); Major General of U.S. Army (1814-1821)
POLITICAL PARTY:	Democratic

OFFICES HELD: Solicitor of Western District of North Carolina;
                       Delegate to Tennessee State Constitutional
                       Convention; Member of U.S. House of
                       Representatives; U.S. Senator; Tennessee
                       Supreme Court judge; Governor of Florida
                       Territory

AGE AT INAUGURATION: 61

TERMS SERVED: Two (1829-1833) (1833-1837)

VICE PRESIDENT: John C. Calhoun (1829-1832, resigned) and
                       Martin Van Buren (1833-1837)

DIED: June 8, 1845, Nashville, Tennessee, age 78

CAUSE OF DEATH: Natural causes

Detail Area

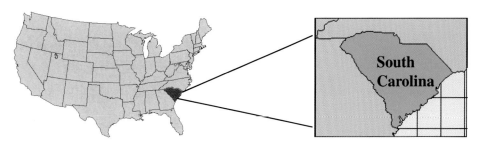

Birthplace of Andrew Jackson

Early Years

*A*ndrew Jackson was born in the Waxhaw region of South Carolina on March 15, 1767. His parents, Andrew Sr. and Elizabeth, and two older brothers, Hugh and Robert, moved there from Ireland only two years earlier. At this time, South Carolina was one of 13 British colonies.

Andrew's father died just before Andrew was born. His mother moved them in with other family.

Andrew was a wild child. He was a bully and had a bad temper, but he protected younger kids and he was honest.

Andrew loved riding horses, playing games, running races, and wrestling. He liked to **compete** with others. Young Andrew learned to read books and was very smart.

In 1775, the colonies began to fight a war against England. It was called the American Revolution. Andrew was only nine, but he wanted to fight for his country.

Andrew Jackson with his horse

A Boy Goes to War

*I*n 1780, when Andrew was only 13, he joined the army so he could fight in the American Revolution. His older brothers, Hugh and Robert, fought in it as well. Hugh was killed during the war.

In 1781, British soldiers attacked Andrew and other colonists in a cabin. Andrew refused to **surrender**. The soldiers put him, his brother, and others in prison!

Andrew and Robert were very sick with **smallpox**. Andrew's mother pleaded with the English to let her sons go. Finally, they traded them for English prisoners.

After the long trip back home, Robert died from illness. Andrew was very sick, but his mother nursed him back to health. Then she nursed other sick people. She died of **cholera** in 1781.

At age 14, Andrew was all alone. He tried living with relatives. He tried working in an uncle's shop, but he was not happy. He ran away with a group of boys.

Andrew went back to school for a while. He even tried teaching, but he did not like it. Finally, he realized he needed to do something with his life. In 1784, he decided to go to Salisbury, North Carolina, and become a lawyer.

Andrew Jackson as a soldier

A Wife and a New Life

*A*ndrew Jackson studied law for four years. He worked very hard, but he still liked to stay out late and act wild.

Andrew got his law license in 1787. One year later, he went to Tennessee and began his practice. At this time, Tennessee was as far west as the colonies reached. The land was wild, like Andrew!

Andrew lived in a boardinghouse owned by the Donelson family. A boardinghouse is a kind of hotel. There, he met Rachel Donelson Robards. They fell in love and were married in 1791.

As a lawyer, Andrew won most of his cases. Many people paid him with land or slaves. He owned a big **plantation** near Nashville, Tennessee. He called it the Hermitage.

Rachel Jackson

The Making of the 7th United States President

1767
Born March 15 in the Waxhaw region of South Carolina

1780
Joins the army to fight in the American Revolution

1781
Andrew and brother put in prison by British troops; they catch small pox and are released

1784
Begins law school at Salisbury, North Carolina

1787
Earns license to practice law

1797
Elected to the Senate

1798
Becomes a judge for the Supreme Court of Tennessee

1802
Elected Major General of the Militia

1804
Resigns from Tennessee Supreme Court

1810
Adopts nephew and names him Andrew Jackson, Jr.

1824
Runs for president but loses to John Quincy Adams

1828
Rachel Jackson dies of heart attack

1828
Elected president of the U.S.

1829
March 4 moves into White House

1831
Many Native American Sauk people killed at the Battle of Bad Ax

PRESIDENTIAL

Andrew Jackson

"There are no necessary evils in government. Its evils exist only in its abuses."

1789
Becomes prosecuting attorney for Nashville

1791
Marries Rachel Donelson Robards

1796
Elected to Congress

Historical Highlights
during Jackson Administration

- Whig party formed

- Texas declares independence from Mexico, the siege of the Alamo

- Samuel Morse invents the telegraph

- States of Arkansas and Michigan admitted to the Union

1812
Fights in the War of 1812, nicknamed "Old Hickory"

1814
Fights in Battle of Horseshoe Bend

1815
Defeats British in the Battle of New Orleans

1832
President Jackson re-elected for second term

1835
Native American Seminole people move from Florida

1837
Andrew Jackson retires as president in March

1838
Native American Cherokee people move from GA to OK along "Trail of Tears"

1845
June 8 Jackson dies at home in Tennessee

YEARS

Judge and Soldier

*I*n 1796, Andrew Jackson was elected to the U.S. Congress. They helped decide laws for the country. Soon he was bored and quit in 1798.

Andrew was a **Supreme Court** judge in Tennessee for six years. Then he went back to work on his **plantation**. Andrew and Rachel adopted their nephew in 1810.

Andrew also fought in duels! One time he was shot near the heart. The bullet stayed in his chest for the rest of his life.

When Andrew was 45, he fought in the War of 1812. He led men in many big battles in the South. He was tough, and his men called him "Old Hickory."

Many Native Americans, angry that American settlers had taken their land, fought with the English against the U.S. in the War of 1812. Andrew Jackson fought many battles against Native Americans.

In 1814, Andrew won the Battle of Horseshoe Bend in Alabama against Native Americans known as the Creeks. He was **promoted** to major general and was put in charge of a huge army.

Major General Andrew Jackson was called "Old Hickory" by his troops.

A War Hero's Campaign

*A*fter winning the Battle of Horseshoe Bend, Andrew was ordered to defend the city of New Orleans in Louisiana. There, he gathered a new group of soldiers. Some were freed slaves, some were Native Americans, some were pirates.

On Januray 8, 1815, Andrew and his men fought the British in the Battle of New Orleans. Over 2,000 English soldiers were hurt or killed. Jackson lost only 71 men. The great victory made Jackson a war hero.

In 1817, Andrew went to Alabama and Georgia to defend settlers against attacks by Native Americans known as the Seminoles. In 1818, he captured Pensacola, Florida, from the British. When Florida became a state in 1821, Andrew was made a governor.

In 1824, Andrew ran for president, but he lost to John Quincy Adams. Right away, Andrew planned his next **campaign**.

When others **campaigned**, they made speeches, visited people, or wrote letters about their ideas. Andrew and his friends wrote songs and sayings. They made buttons and drew signs. They even made hickory canes! Nobody had ever done these things before.

Many new states were joining the United States. There were more voters than ever before! In November 1828, Andrew Jackson won the election. He became the 7th president of the United States.

Andrew Jackson in battle

President Jackson

*I*n December 1828, Rachel Jackson died. Andrew was very sad. His niece Emily took over the work that the president's wife did.

Andrew Jackson was 61 when he moved into the White House in 1829. Many people came to the White House to cheer for their hero. The crowds were so large, Andrew had to escape through a side door.

Andrew gave government jobs to many in his own **party**. Many presidents do this when they're elected. It is called the "spoils system."

Andrew also sought help from a small group of friends who were not even in **politics**. They came to White House meetings through the back door. They were called the "Kitchen Cabinet."

While Andrew Jackson was president, Cherokee, Choctaw, Creek, and other Native Americans lost more and more land to the United States. President Jackson passed laws forcing thousands of Native Americans to leave their lands and move further west.

Andrew Jackson

In 1832, Andrew ran for president once more. He **campaigned** against big banks that controlled the nation's money. He believed that this control would hurt America's businesses.

After winning the election, Andrew worked hard to be an active leader. He felt that the president should be more responsible for the nation's good.

Andrew often disagreed with **Congress**, and used his **veto** power to stop new laws from being passed. This hard work gave the **presidency** more and more power. It also set a good example for future presidents.

*Opposite page:
Andrew Jackson
as president*

Old Soldier

Andrew Jackson retired as president in March 1837. He was 70 years old. He went home to the Hermitage.

Andrew was sick. He had a lung disease called **tuberculosis**. He ached from old wounds.

But Andrew remained active. He rode horses. He looked over his **plantation** every day.

Andrew also helped with the **campaigns** of friends who ran for president. And he wrote letters.

On June 8, 1845, Andrew Jackson died. He was 78 years old. He was buried at the Hermitage next to his wife Rachel.

Opposite page: Andrew Jackson's home, the Hermitage, where he and his wife are buried

A Man of the People

•Andrew Jackson's parents came from Ireland. They told him and his brothers many stories about being treated unfairly by the English. Andrew grew up wanting to fight for the "common people." Even as president, he tried to think about what ordinary people needed.

•When Andrew Jackson was only 13, British soldiers captured him and other colonists during the American Revolution. An English leader ordered Andrew to clean the mud off the Englishman's boots. Andrew refused! The English soldier cut Andrew with his sword. Andrew had scars for the rest of his life.

•Andrew Jackson could be tough. He once punished soldiers by hanging them. A leader once said, "If Andrew Jackson starts talking about hanging people, you better go out and find some rope."

•Andrew Jackson loved Rachel very much. After she died, he wore a locket with her picture around his neck everywhere he went.

Andrew Jackson being addressed as Old Hickory

Glossary

Campaign—the work done to get people to vote for someone.

Cholera—a painful stomach disease.

College—a school you can go to after high school.

Compete—to try to beat another person at a race or game.

Declaration of Independence—an important paper that said the English colonies wanted to be free and start their own government.

Party—a group of people organized to gain political power.

Politics—the process of making laws and running a government.

Plantation—a big farm, usually with crops like tobacco or cotton and farmed by slaves.

Presidency—the job of being president.

Promote—to give someone a higher rank or job.

Smallpox—a disease that causes fever and a rash of sores.

Supreme Court—the highest court in the United States, or in each state.

Surrender—to give up.

Tuberculosis—a lung disease that was common in the 1800s; it killed many people.

Veto—the right or power to forbid or stop.

Internet Sites

Welcome to the White House
www.whitehouse.gov

Visit the official Web site of the White House. There is an introduction from the United State's current president. Also included is extensive biographies of each president, White House history information, art in the White House, First Ladies, and First Families. Visit the section titled: The White House for Kids, where kids can become more active in the government of the United States.

Presidents of the United States – Potus
www.ipl.org/ref/POTUS/

This excellent Web site has background information and biographies on each president. Also included are results of every presidential election, cabinet members, presidency highlights, and some fun facts on each of the presidents. Links to historical documents, audio and video files, and other presidential sites are also included to enrich this site.

Home of Andrew Jackson
www.thehermitage.com/

Visit the home of President Jackson, known as The Hermitage, at this wonderful Web site. Included in this site are photos, an in depth biography of Andrew Jackson, fun facts, a virtual tour of the home of President Jackson, and much more.

These sites are subject to change. Go to your favorite search engine and type in United States presidents for more sites.

Pass It On

History Enthusiasts: educate readers around the country by passing on information you've learned about presidents or other important people who've changed history. Share your little-known facts and interesting stories. We want to hear from you!

To get posted on the ABDO Publishing Company Web site, E-mail us at "History@abdopub.com"

Visit the ABDO Publishing Company Web site at www.abdopub.com

Index